lookin

CORN

churches

Joanna Mattingly

Dedication:
To Eleanor and Clara, and in memory of their brother Alexander

First published 2005

Tor Mark Press P O Box 4
Redruth Cornwall TR16 5YX

Designed by Alix Wood, Bodmin

Printed by R Booth Ltd
Antron Hill, Mabe, Penryn TR10 9HH

ISBN 0 85025 404 3

Front Cover: Morwenstow

Title page: Mabe

Inside Back Cover: North Tamerton

Back Cover: Advent

looking at cornish churches

Churches are a major feature of the landscape in Cornwall. Few parish churches are in villages or towns because Cornwall is predominantly a land of hamlets and farms. Cornish churches often sit at the centre of a web of church paths. These paths linked the 'church town' (often no more than one or two houses) to other settlements and farms in the parish, with the pathways often marked by wayside crosses. Oval churchyards or 'lans', churchyard crosses, lop-sided church plans, tall towers, granite walls and piers are common, while holy wells indicate other former religious sites where there were once chapels too. The Cornish religious landscape was peppered with chapels in much the same way that Methodist chapels abound today. Also most Cornish parishes, unlike the rest of the country, bear the name of their church saint. Some of these saints are unique to Cornwall and this, like the 'lans', reflects Cornwall's distinctive early Christian heritage.

St Dennis hillfort site and church path. The original saint here is not known and St Dennis appears to derive from the Cornish word Dinas meaning castle.

Introduction

Looking at Churches focuses on those Cornish churches first built between 450 and 1,000 years ago. This period is considered here to be medieval but excludes the most distinctive 'Celtic' phase of Cornish Christianity before 1000 AD when place-names were formulated, oval churchyards constructed and memorial stones erected. Church buildings in Cornwall span the period from just before the Norman Conquest to the present day. For most of this time Cornwall was part of the diocese of Exeter. A separate Cornish diocese may have been intended in the century before the Norman Conquest but Exeter diocese had superseded this by 1050. Cornwall was probably considered to be too small an area to have its own diocese, and it was only in 1877 that the first bishop of Truro was appointed.

Terwick in Sussex at dusk
an example of a simple chancel, nave and bell turret church.

Cornwall's medieval churches are not simple buildings, contrary to popular belief, and most have been altered many times. Cornwall was a wealthy county in the late medieval period, not an economic backwater. It was on the western fringes of the West Country cloth-making area, and had in addition, great tin and fish resources. Much of this wealth, particularly from the tin industry, was invested in church building even as the major religious changes, known as the Reformation, occurred. Today only two Cornish churches (St John near Antony and Tremaine) can truly be called simple. For clusters of simple churches one has to go to the poorer parts of Gloucestershire, Hampshire, Sussex, Surrey, Kent, Yorkshire or other Midlands and northern counties.

Every church rebuilding led to architectural losses as well as gains and the best parallels for Cornish churches can now be found in Devon, and to a lesser extent in Somerset, Dorset, Gloucestershire and Wiltshire. However, the largest late medieval Cornish churches tend to have no clerestories (additional high windows above the nave arcades) and hence the body of the church is lower and architecturally less-ambitious than those in other south-west counties.

St Enodoc chapel *showing south aisle, chancel, nave and transeptal tower with spire. This is one of many examples of a lop-sided church plan.*

Parish churches and chapels

Parish churches were distinguished more clearly from chapels when each diocese was divided into parishes. Only parish churches after 1300 were able to baptise and bury, whereas previously important chapels had had fonts and cemeteries too. In Cornwall there were originally about 170 parish churches. Many of these carefully preserved their Norman fonts as a 'title deed' to their parish status, which may be why so many Norman fonts survive. During the medieval period some newer chapels, especially in towns, were allowed to have fonts and burial grounds on payment of a fee to their mother church. Few became parishes in the medieval period and most had to wait until the nineteenth century. Of Cornwall's 212 medieval churches, St Enodoc and St Michael Porthilly are still chapels of St Minver parish and St Nectan a chapelry of St Winnow.

aRChitectuRal peRiods

Some architectural knowledge will greatly enhance any church visit. The main periods of architecture that relate to Cornwall are:

The *Romanesque* or *Norman* period, which started with the Norman Conquest of 1066 and continued for some time after 1200. Round arches are typical of the Romanesque style (as of earlier 'Roman' architecture and also the last phases of Perpendicular Gothic as shown below).

Gothic architecture with pointed arches gradually replaced the Romanesque. One reason was that less stone was required for Gothic than Romanesque architecture due to European advances in engineering. Changes within the Gothic period itself appear to be due to the need to provide larger and larger frames for stained glass windows.

Tremaine *one of Cornwall's two simplest churches, north wall showing small Romanesque window and door.*

Cullompton church in Devon *interior view showing clerestory, angel roof and rood screen. Clerestories are rare, and generally early, features in Devon too.*

The Gothic period can be divided into three parts. The *Early English* period began before 1250 and continued for some time after 1300 in Cornwall. Single slit windows, known as lancets, are among the features of this first Gothic phase. Square-headed windows may also occur later in this period and the next. The *Decorated* period, or second Gothic phase, in Cornwall started about 1320–30 and continued to 1450 at least (rather later than many other places). Larger windows, sometimes with geometric tracery, and pointed arches are common in this phase.

The *Perpendicular* period, or last and longest phase of Gothic, began about 1450 and continued as late as the 1660s in Cornwall. Pointed arches in this period were usually four-centred (drawn using four compass points, two for each side). With engineering advances, this arch-type tended to flatten out, and round-headed arches are also

Ruan Minor *south wall of transept with original Early English lancet (single light) windows.*

Padstow *south chapel of church with flamboyant-style early fifteenth century (four light) windows.*

Camborne *north aisle and late Perpendicular (four light) windows of 1538–40s date. This shows flatter headed windows occupying larger areas of wall.*

found again by the Tudor period (1485–1603). Perpendicular church windows often occupy more space than the wall between. They also include square-headed mullions, which look like house windows.

Dating church features to one of these periods is often difficult as older forms, like ogees (reversed 'S' shapes), could continue in use or be revived. Sometimes materials give a clue to date as shaped granite is rare before the Perpendicular period.

Detail of St Endelienta's tomb St Endellion showing typical ogee arch. This Catacleuse shrine is of late fifteenth century date and is Perpendicular, not Decorated as might have been expected.

Cornwall's religious houses

Cornwall is not generally regarded as a county of monasteries like Yorkshire. There were no great abbeys here, and Cornwall's five major religious houses at Bodmin, St Germans, Glasney, Launceston, and Tywardreath were, with the exception of Glasney, all Norman priories (priories being smaller versions of abbeys). Glasney College near Penryn was a college of canons modelled on Exeter Cathedral and founded in 1265. There were about a dozen smaller religious houses, two friaries and some hospitals and almshouses. Recent excavations show that Glasney College was Exeter's architectural equivalent and hence Cornwall's most significant Decorated period building. It was designed, like Exeter, by Thomas of Witney and the *Ordinalia* and other medieval Cornish religious plays appear to have been written here. Some medieval religious houses, including Bodmin and St Germans, had been monastic sites before 1066.

During periods of architectural change, two styles may be used together and new styles may have been used first at important places including Cornwall's monastic churches which are now mainly lost.

Church detectives must beware of *Georgian* church restoration, now mostly gone without trace. Wooden 'sash' windows were put into many Cornish churches, particularly in storm-blown Penwith, in the period 1750 to 1837. *Victorian* restorers removed these and sometimes tried to 'early-up' a church with guess-work lancets or Decorated style windows. This was most common in Victorian church restoration of the 1850s to 1870s.

View of Launceston from the castle. This shows the church of St Stephen (the original monastic site) on the hill, while the smaller church of St Thomas in the valley to the left marks the site of the medieval priory.

Paul church interior view of north chapel showing Georgian-style window and Godolphin family armour.

Medieval churches were originally built for Catholic not Protestant worship. Put simply, medieval Catholic worship was based on prayers and processions, which tended to lead to church enlargement – the creation of altar spaces for more prayers and religious services, and processional aisles. By contrast, Protestant worship was based on preaching and, to a lesser extent, communion, and this required only a wide nave and chancel. This plainer approach to religion led to the replacement of figurative painting with painted texts and encouraged the 'fossilisation' of existing church fabric. In Cornwall, abandoned building projects can often be identified, because many Cornish churches were still being enlarged as Protestantism became the official religion.

North Petherwin's fossilised north side A lean-to Norman aisle and clerestory appear in the foreground and the 1518–24 north chapel, beyond the north porch, in the background. School-children from the local primary school are re-enacting the annual custom (recorded in 1490s and later church accounts here) of meting or measuring the church with candlewick. Once the circuit was completed the candlewick would be cut up into shorter lengths and used to make the candles needed by the church for the next year.

how churches were used

The way in which churches were used affected their form and later development. Churches began as buildings with open spaces without any seats or screens. Each church had a chancel for the priest and a nave for the people. The chancel arch divided the chancel from the nave. The altar was at the east end of the chancel and the font near the west end of the nave, often between the south and north doors, where two doors existed. Only major churches had aisles or transepts added (for processions and extra altars). Worship was simple but might include plain chant (un-accompanied singing), and people stood or sat on the floor.

All this changed at the end of the Romanesque and start of the Gothic period. Christ was now thought to be present during church services. Priests were no longer allowed to marry and the holiest parts of the church (chancel, east ends of aisles and transepts) were screened off with stone screens. Fonts were also provided with lockable covers so that the holy water could not be taken away for non-religious

Breton procession at St Day near Gwennap, 2000 A new Breton statue of St Day is being carried. It is not clear if there really was a Cornish St Day as this Cornish chapel was dedicated to Trinity (Day perhaps being a corruption of this). Links between medieval Brittany and Cornwall were strong, with Breton craftsmen working at North Petherwin and Bodmin in the early sixteenth century.

St Ive triple sedilia with piscina or drain constructed in the east wall of the chancel.

purposes. Each altar now needed a piscina or drain because people believed that Christ's blood (the contents of the chalice or priest's cup) had to return to the earth.

Many clergy had to extend their chancels further east to accommodate triple sedilia or seats. In many parts of England, but not Cornwall, chancels of this period are higher and more impressive that the rest of the church. This was because, in Cornwall, it was the people rather than the clergy who paid most for church building. Sedilia provided seating for the priest and his helpers (clerks who had not yet become priests), and sometimes wall and pillar plinths were made for weak, sick or old people to sit on in the nave. The phrase 'the weakest go to the wall' appears to derive from this.

Worship by 1300 often included processions and prayers for the dead. A demand for daily services led to the building of 'chapels of ease' (ease meaning greater convenience in this case)

Cotehele house chapel with Breton-style bell turret. The north wall, shown here, may be from the original 1411 chapel but the bell turret is part of the late fifteenth or early sixteenth century remodelling.

especially in towns and gentry homes. Processions around the church before the Sunday service and on feast days now included a processional cross and sometimes banners and flags. New aisles were built to accommodate these spectacles and existing aisles had to be widened and heightened. Older doorways were sometimes deliberately recycled when walls were rebuilt further out. This helps to account for the survival of so many Norman doorways in Cornwall, and suggests that such features retained their meaning and were respected by later generations. Norman fonts were similarly preserved in large numbers in Cornwall.

Blisland south aisle roof angel (re-sited).

The churches of the period can now be seen as 'factories' where prayers were made. Prayers were needed to shorten the period of time people expected to spend in Purgatory – the pools of ice and rivers of fire that lay between Heaven and Hell. Indulgences, or pardons, could be purchased from several Cornish churches to lessen the time spent in Purgatory. Money raised from these indulgences was usually ploughed back into building projects at these same churches. Angels were included in many of Cornwall's wagon roofs to represent heaven. Chantries were also set up by

Chantries

Chantries were private screened-off east-facing spaces. They housed extra altars and priests needed for increased prayer production (each priest was only allowed to say one mass a day). Chantry chapels were also used as private burial places by the gentry, the most impressive being at St Columb Major, Duloe and Padstow.

gentry families in newly built chancel chapels or transepts.

Those parishioners of more moderate wealth joined religious groups known as guilds. These 'corporate' chantries often had their own altars and charged a membership fee. At St Thomas's Launceston, new guild members gave a lamb worth nine old pennies to the guild of All Hallows. In addition to guilds, two or three individuals might pay for a light to

Sithney north chapel. *The degree of ornamentation over the east window here is suggestive of a gentry chantry and is similar to Cury and Padstow.*

Botus Fleming *south aisle and nave showing image brackets. That on the second pillar has a canopy and is especially elaborate.*

burn before a statue of a saint in the nave. There were also groups of young men, young women and wives in most parishes who lit candles before these and other images.

With all these parish groups, Cornish churches could easily have five or more altars, and many more images (both statues and wall paintings). Some altars and images would have been located in the nave and aisles. Public space within the church was consequently being reduced as each new altar had to be screened-off. Across the full-width of the church, separating chancel and chantry chapels, from nave and aisles was the rood screen. This was so called because it supported the great rood or crucifix with attendant figures of the Virgin Mary and St John the Evangelist.

Over time these wooden rood screens with decorated ceilures or ceilings overhead replaced the chancel arch as the dividing marker between the people's church and that of the clergy and gentry. In Cornwall, only Towednack retains its early chancel arch; elsewhere such arches were generally swept away during the great Perpendicular rebuilding when continuous roofs were introduced.

Lanreath rood screen and panelled chancel roof. It seems likely that only chancels and ceilures may have been panelled originally, with plain roof timbers on show elsewhere in the church. The loft has gone but would originally have run along the top of the screen.

Creed view from south aisle across nave to north transept. A 'creep' hole has been cut through the arcade wall and the upper doorway of the rood stair can be seen in the background. The base of the screen survives and includes grotesque monsters in its carving.

North Tamerton church and church house in churchyard. This church house has lost part of its upper storey and its external stair, perhaps when converted to a dwelling house. A less altered Cornish church house can be seen at Poundstock. Note the imposing three-stage (storey) unbuttressed tower and how the body of the church barely comes up to the first stage. This vertical proportion of one-third church to two-thirds tower is typical of Perpendicular churches in Cornwall and Devon. Unbuttressed towers were cheaper to build than buttressed ones and it seems that most buttresses were added for show.

Rood lofts, wide jettied-out platforms on top of the rood screens, became necessary in the very late fifteenth and early sixteenth century when music was introduced into Cornish churches. Such lofts housed singers and the church organ, worked by bellows. Stairs were built in the north or south wall of the church to reach these lofts. Stairs 'going nowhere' and 'creep' holes (which once allowed people access along the whole length of the loft) above the

Church Houses

Church houses once existed in almost every parish in southern England and Wales. The main Whitsun church ale was brewed in a ground floor room by the young men of the parish from ingredients provided by the parishioners. The parishioners then paid to attend the feast in the large first floor hall, money being raised for church funds in the process. These high quality buildings were often built at the cost of the parishioners on the edge of churchyards by the same masons who built the church (they were not built purposely to house the masons). After church ales were banned at the Reformation in 1548 several became poorhouses, schools and pubs. In Devon church house inns are commonly found near the church.

nave arcades are often all that remain to show where the rood screen once stood.

Church feasts, which included ale drinkings, were once held in churches. Official church disapproval of such secular activities and the fact that naves and aisles were beginning to fill up with altars, statues, pulpits and pews, led to church feasts being held in purpose-built church houses. Pulpits and pews were introduced relatively late (the 1490s being the earliest recorded in Cornwall at Bodmin) as the fashion for sermons grew.

Other features of the late medieval church interior include Easter sepulchres (representing Christ's tomb), which were usually sited on the north side of the chancel. These were only used during Easter week when a crucifix was symbolically 'buried' there to represent Christ's burial and Resurrection. Trusted parishioners 'watched' (guarded) the Easter Sepulchre (and the parish silver) from Maundy Thursday to Easter day in return for food and drink. In Cornwall the tombs of wealthy gentry or the parish saint were commonly sited on this side of the chancel too and some doubled as the Easter sepulchre.

Many more Cornish churches claimed, with some justification, to have the bones of their patron saints than anywhere elsewhere in England. Local pilgrimage to neighbouring shrines was very popular (and easy) in Cornwall, but Cornish men and women also found their way to Hailes in Gloucestershire, Windsor in

Lanteglos-by-Fowey Mohun tomb. *Although this is located in the south aisle, rather than the north side of the chancel, a painting of Christ standing in his tomb on the back wall suggests that this was the Easter Sepulchre too.*

Berkshire, and further afield to Rome and the Holy Land.

Moving to external church features, porches first appear in the Gothic period and were built in part as 'wedding marquees' according to the historian Christopher Brooke. People were married at the church door, the marriage contract might be sealed in a room over the porch (where

Bodmin church *view of west end and south aisle showing three-storey porch. Most church porches had no chambers over.*

one existed) and the couple then entered the church to attend a special wedding mass. Porches often contained stoups for holy water with which the parishioners would be sprinkled at service time. Towers housed the church bells, and occasionally a first-floor chapel. They were symbols of parish pride and this may account for the large numbers of imposing towers in Cornwall. Battlements were usually found only on church towers and porches but larger churches sometimes decorated their show front with this feature.

By the later medieval period, people's lives revolved more and more around their church. Churches were the television of their age, providing music, drama, sport and entertainment as well as religion. Religious plays were performed in Cornish and English (at a time when church services were all in Latin) in open-air playing places to raise funds for church works. Football and other games, including hurling (the Cornish national sport), were encouraged by the church on Shrove Tuesday as a way of letting off steam before Lent began. Churches in Cornwall, as elsewhere, were also art galleries and museums at a time when very few people had paintings on their walls. Much of this art has been lost with walls reverting to being blank canvases again. In the case of stained glass (with the notable exception of St Neot) all that survives is the frame.

church Building – materials, method and design

The earliest surviving stone church wall in Cornwall (part of Minster) may date from about 1000 or a century later. During this period and the Romanesque, thick rubble walls were built from local stone. Granite was only used in moorland parishes where pieces of manageable size could be found. Norman walls are generally battered out (thickened at the bottom) to make them more stable, but could be quite tall. Wooden scaffolding was used to construct walls then as later. Fonts, doorways and other features were carved from better quality stone. Carvable limestone and lime (for mortar) had to be brought in by sea, river and road (Cornwall has little or no native limestone). North Cornish slate was used for most church roofs. Windows were small because glass was expensive. As glass became cheaper, windows became larger.

Churches were built to a plan. The simplest plan was a single cell or chancel type, commonly used for medieval chapels. Churches were built with a chancel and a nave at least. The chancel could have a round or square east end, and some churches had narrow side aisles added to them as well. In the Early English and Decorated periods many transepts were also added to Cornish churches. More than half of all Cornish churches, and several Devon churches, had a cross-shaped or cruciform plan at one time. Towers could be central, north, south, west or even separate

Blisland *west end showing 'battered out' (buttressed) Norman wall at west end of nave and later granite ashlar Perpendicular south aisle in foreground.*

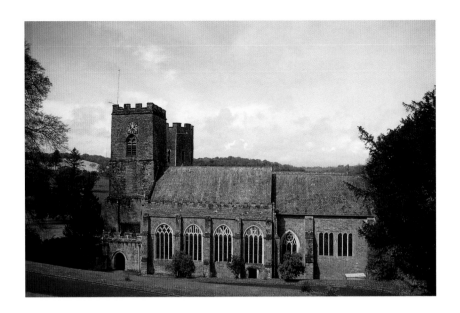

from the church, as at Gunwalloe. Over twenty Cornish towers are not at the west end of the church. Non-west towers also occur in Devon, Dorset, Kent and other counties with early church buildings. St Germans, and possibly Liskeard at one time, had two west towers each because they were major churches.

Towers attached to the western end of the nave became more normal and spires were fashionable additions in the Early English and Decorated periods. Some spires were superseded by taller towers later. Cornwall's tallest recorded spire (150 feet including the Norman tower) at Bodmin was struck by lightning in 1699. It was rivalled by the fine

St Germans *south side showing twin towers and parish aisle remodelled in Decorated and Perpendicular periods. Note the Cotehele-style domestic windows at the south chapel end on the right. These may date from the 1540s or even later. The remains of the clerestory are only evident internally now.*

fourteenth century Breton-influenced spire at Lostwithiel. Clerestories (rows of additional high windows above the aisles) are rare in Cornwall because they did not remain fashionable into the Perpendicular period. Remains of a Norman clerestory can be seen at St Germans, early fourteenth century ones survive at Fowey, Lostwithiel and North Petherwin and an early to mid-fifteenth century one at Callington.

Stone-masons were the highest paid craftsmen throughout the medieval period. Their skill can still be seen in the many Norman fonts, doorways, and pier capitals, Early English and Decorated period spires, aisles, geometric windows, piscinas, sedilia and tombs that still survive in Cornwall.

the perpendicular rebuilding of cornish churches

In the Perpendicular period (c1450 on) Cornwall's churches became building sites once more but on a much greater scale than before. Towers, aisles, porches and even new chancels were added to many churches and some churches were totally rebuilt. Other churches had a smooth

Ladock view across church from south aisle to north transept. The middle pier of the transept aligns on the south aisle pier in the foreground. This may represent an aborted aisle.

Tremaine interior looking east. This shows that even Cornwall's simplest church was remodelled with a continuous wagon roof and domestic style east window. There is now no obvious visual break between the chancel at the east end and the nave.

granite skin of large ashlar (smooth-faced rectangular shaped blocks rather than random stone) added to them. Much of this work appears to be later than once thought – several aisles, porches, chancels and some towers date from the 1500s to the 1540s. People in Cornwall simply ignored warnings of religious change and continued to build well into the Reformation period (c1529–70s). The late start of much of this work meant that some planned schemes were never finished.

The typical Perpendicular Cornish church plan has north and south aisles of about the same width and height as nave and chancel, and a west tower. Roofs by the later Perpendicular period were continuous. Seen from the east, there should be a triple row of gables (giving this plan type the name 'three hall church') with the tower about three times the height of the body of the church (e.g. Jacobstow, Stoke Climsland). Additional aisles, chapels or transepts sometimes occur in the richest parishes.

Mabe *east end and west tower. This church is one of many that represents the three hall ideal. However note the smaller chancel window in the centre. This appears to be of Decorated period origin rather than Perpendicular as the aisle windows are.*

The Reformation and church buildings

The English Reformation began in about 1529 and initially affected religious houses more than churches. It was only in 1548, with the abolition of chantries, guilds, colleges, church processions and Purgatory, that the main motivation for all this building work was removed. Church building was given a temporary boost by the return of Catholic worship in 1553–8 and in Cornwall could continue on into the 1560s. Late church building is also documented in the West Country as a whole and other Catholic areas like East Anglia, Cheshire, and Lancashire. Many Cornish churches still show evidence of aborted schemes, for instance pillars in the middle of transepts, passage squints (possibly), lop-sided plans, or beautiful Perpendicular churches with architecturally less imposing or absent towers.

Building extension could start at the east end of the church with holes being knocked through the chancel wall to create an aisle or involve the opening out of a transept. In this latter case a pillar would be placed under the transept arch to line up with a pillar in an existing aisle and work might proceed either west or east. In the former case this could have resulted in an aisle being built and, in the latter, a chancel chapel. At Launceston, the wall of the present church of St Mary Magdalene seems to have been built anti-clockwise around an earlier chapel with space left for a new tower that was never built. In all these cases worship would have continued alongside building work.

Bodmin was one of the first Cornish churches to be built in the new fully-developed Perpendicular style and was very much a prototype for other churches. Pillars and windows were probably based on Devon models. Pentewan stone, quarried near St Austell, was used for the south side and local slate for the less seen north side. Granite came from the St Austell area for the new-style windows and pillars at Bodmin. Work had begun in 1469 on the church's south aisle, and the walls and porch there were built in three years according to existing building accounts. An indulgence, or pardon, obtained by the church in 1475 partly paid for the south aisle roof. By 1494

Bodmin *north chapel exterior with pre-1469 three-light window type, and north aisle with post-1469 four-light windows. The latter became the standard Cornish Perpendicular window frame from their introduction at Bodmin in 1469 until the 1530s or even 1540s. At St Neot, where this window-type occurs c1500, it is possible to see the sort of stained glass pictures (usually individual saints) that these windows once framed.*

Bodmin's north side had been completed too. Only the Norman west door and north tower with mid-Gothic spire remained of the old church by 1500.

At North Petherwin, a rural parish formerly in Devon, the south chapel was built in the 1490s, the south aisle in 1505–7 and the north chapel in 1518–24 together with a rood screen and loft. A north aisle was planned but never built because of the Reformation.

Other major churches like St Kew and St Neot added first a south and then a north aisle in the period from the 1480s to the 1540s. Window and pillar types are similar to those found earlier at Bodmin, but roofs are now continuous. The speed of building at each place depended on how quickly people could raise the money. Bodmin was the richest town in Cornwall. Poorer places in the county might have taken longer than ten years to build an aisle. Often there were large gaps between aisle building campaigns. Dendrochronology (tree ring dating) at St Veep recently showed that the north aisle there was built in the 1540s some eighty years after the south aisle and nave.

North Petherwin *south aisle pier of Cornish standard type. This pier was brought from Hingston Down near Callington, a thirty mile round trip. The south aisle was completed in 1507 with a granite pier and respond (half pier at the end of the aisle) from Rough Tor on Bodmin Moor thus saving five miles on each return trip. Cornish standard Perpendicular piers with four attached shafts, hollow chamfers (to remove angles) between, and individual capitals to the shafts occur at Bodmin in 1469, although of earlier origin.*

St Veep exterior view of west end and tower. The earlier aisle is to the right.

More ambitious schemes with exterior carving took longer and seem to have been sixteenth century phenomena as in Devon. None of these schemes was ever fully implemented because of the Reformation. Truro St Mary's south aisle (now part of the cathedral) took fourteen years from 1504 to 1518 to complete and seems to have been the model for a thirty-two year, or more, complete rebuild at Launceston St Mary Magdalene. Building of this most ambitious of all granite churches began in 1511 with the south porch, every possible surface was carved like 'a Fair Isle jumper' in stone, and a surviving inscription suggests that the church was built anti-clockwise, finishing at the north door. Neither Truro nor Launceston ever installed grand towers as they may have planned to do. At Launceston a gap had been left for this tower between the west wall of the church and the old tower. After the Reformation, two shops filled the gap, and later a vestry was built in the space. By contrast, at Probus, perhaps the finest tower in Cornwall (based on a Somerset model) was begun in 1520, but the motivation to update the church to the same fancy design went out with the Reformation.

Launceston St Mary Magdalene detail of granite carving above the priest's door in the south chapel.

Probus tower top two stages (floors) of three-stage Somerset tower.

Not every church was in a rush to add aisles. At Egloshayle, by Wadebridge, the church was still cruciform as late as 1529 and at least three Cornish churches remain cruciform today. The south aisle at Egloshayle was added from 1529 to the early 1530s and the new chancel window made to match the east window of that aisle. A north chapel was planned but had to be abandoned for the usual reasons. Its fossilised remains show that work here was being done from west to east. A curious passage squint at Cury may also represent the start of a south aisle there. Money was left for this as late as 1543 and the church is unusual in having two rood stairs. Pillars in the middle of transepts in a number of Cornish churches could also represent aisles that were planned but never built.

Granite was the main Perpendicular building material. It is a firm, stable and plentiful stone and so was used for most outside walls, piers, window frames and doorways. Given its

Egloshayle view of interior of south aisle looking east to distinctive 1529 east window. Similar windows can be seen at St Erth, Lanlivery (1520), and Padstow.

load-bearing properties, it is strange that no clerestories were built in Cornwall at this period. Bodmin Moor quarries, including Rough Tor, are first noted in 1507–9 but moorland tors elsewhere were being quarried already by the second half of the fifteenth century. Parishes near the quarry sites took advantage of the fact that granite splits easily into regular blocks, and they built impressive ashlar walls with it. Other parishes were prepared to travel thirty miles or more on a return journey with horse-drawn sledges to obtain their granite monolith (single block) piers. More easily worked stone like Polyphant or greenstone was sometimes used for piers and other features early on but supplies were more limited and did not weather well externally. Catacleuse, a type of greenstone from St Merryn parish, was used for the finest Perpendicular carving – apostle fonts, angel corbels and saints' shrines. It can resemble cast iron at first glance.

Cury passage squint and rood stair. With the building of a second rood stair on the north side of the church, this earlier stair had become redundant.

St Merryn Cornish standard piers of the south aisle with single Devon-style capitals. Note the crispness of carving in Catacleuse compared to granite.

After 1548, active building seems to have been mostly confined to Stratton hundred. This area was the poorest and most northerly part of Cornwall. It also lies furtherest from good granite sources; the nearest being Bodmin Moor. Much building work is documented in churchwardens' accounts at Poughill and Stratton in the 1540s, while a 1564 date occurs on the south aisle at Morwenstow and 1567 on the porch at Kilkhampton. Occasionally major work is documented later still. For example, the north chapel at Calstock was built around 1585–8, Paul church had to be rebuilt after 1595 (except the tower), the tower of St Teath church is dated 1630, and the last Perpendicular church was built at Falmouth in 1662 and later.

Morwenstow south side and tower in late afternoon sun. Note that the south aisle window is the same as that used at Falmouth a hundred years later.

important moments in cornish church history

Christianity probably came to Cornwall in the fifth or early sixth centuries. This was five hundred years before stone churches became common. Inscribed memorial stones (of wealthy Christian landowners), monastic sites with oval enclosures, wooden churches (possibly) and Hiberno-Saxon (also known as 'Celtic') churchyard crosses partly fill the five hundred year gap. Cornish churches were part of a rich religious landscape of lesser chapels (including several of 1000 or earlier origin), some with holy wells (actually springs), crosses, sanctuary markers, holy paths, holy trees and even saintly footprints. Holy wells, sometimes with elaborate well-houses of Perpendicular date, are a particular feature of Cornish parishes with more than one holy well per parish being common.

Their present isolation is misleading as they were always companions to chapels or parish churches providing holy water for the font and stoup, or curative waters

Towan holy well in St Austell parish, detail of medieval corbel (statue bracket) picked out in luminous moss, and vaulted roof. The well-house covered a square stone basin into which the original spring ran.

St Agnes's footprint (filled with water) beside path leading from church to the chapel and holy well sites above Chapel Porth.

for sick people and animals. Crosses survive in even larger numbers than wells, but saints' footprints along with the greener than normal holy paths and holy trees are largely gone.

Norman origins are likely for about 140 Cornish churches with the rest being Early English in origin. The parish system was in place by 1300 when Cornwall had about 170 parishes. Some forty chapels became parish churches later. Parishioners were expected to support the church with a tenth of their produce (crops, animals and animal products like butter, and fish mainly). Religious houses in Cornwall and elsewhere often took their cut too from parish church money. This process was known as appropriation and was common before the Black Death. The religious house took all of the

Rectors, vicars and curates

Originally the incumbent or main priest of each parish church was known as the rector. Where a parish was appropriated, the religious house became the rector, and a deputy or vicar was appointed to take church services. The vicar's salary came from the lesser tithes (animals and their produce mainly). In the case of chapels, curates were paid by rectors (whether heads of religious houses or the local parish priest) to 'serve the cure'. Many churches and chapels had additional priests employed by gentry and parishioners to serve chantry chapels. Men usually became priests between the ages of 24 and 26.

great tithes on arable crops (the most valuable tithes) and this meant that a great deal of money left Cornwall.

The Black Death of 1349–50, which is now thought to have killed half to two-thirds of the population in Cornwall as elsewhere, had less effect on churches than once thought. The main result was a great shortage of priests, and a huge demand for them. Although the population did not recover fully until the 1550s or later, some Cornish churches were being enlarged again by 1400. After 1500 much of this new work was funded by the Cornish tin industry. Cloth, fishing, farming and trade also paid for Cornish church building.

The Reformation began about 1529 but had little effect on parish churches at first. In 1538 some images were removed and in 1548 chalices and church plate that had been used at the extra altars was taken away and melted down. This, and the new church services in English not Latin, pushed many Cornish people to

rebel against King Edward VI's government in 1548 and 1549.

The Prayer Book Rebellion of 1549 demonstrated the strength of Catholic faith in Cornwall and Devon at this time with several clergy involved. In 1553–8

Hailes Abbey *Gloucestershire, detail of cloister with defaced angel. Hailes was rector of Breage church and its three chapelries of Cury, Germoe and Gunwalloe from 1246 until 1539.*

Catholic worship started again during the reign of Queen Mary. Statues were put back, lofts replaced, walls repainted, and church ales brewed again in church houses. Then Queen Mary died and the country became Protestant again, though more slowly than in the late 1540s and early 1550s. Wooden communion tables replaced altars once more and in the early to mid-1570s communion cups took the place of the remaining medieval chalices. From the 1570s Catholics were known as Recusants and could no longer worship openly.

Iconoclasm (image-breaking or licensed vandalism) was less thorough than in other parts of the country and occurred later. For example, most Cornish stained glass was smashed in 1650–1 during the third English Civil War. Available evidence from documents suggests that this was the work of religious fanatics among the Parliamentarian soldiers not local people.

St Austell church tower detail of west face showing early sixteenth century statues restored to their niches. How these survived the Civil War is unclear, but perhaps they were hidden in the churchyard.

truro cathedral and cornish churches

Church building, with the odd exception – St Charles the Martyr at Falmouth in 1662 and later, and two Georgian rebuilds at Redruth and Helston – really began again in the early nineteenth century. Aisleless 'preaching boxes' were created, for instance at St Martin-in-Meneage. New 'Gothick' churches were built at St Day and on the site of Penzance's medieval chapel of St Mary's in the late 1820s and early 1830s. In 1848, new parishes were created in the mining areas and new churches were built there by William White and other architects.

Truro Cathedral *south aisle exterior of 1501–18 and later of old St Mary's church, looking west.*

Truro Cathedral, in some ways the least Cornish of any Cornish church, was begun in 1880. Some granite was used with Bath stone (limestone) in its construction, but it looks more like a fourteenth century French cathedral, such as Quimper in Brittany. The vertical emphasis of the triple spires and body of the church are completely at odds with the usual horizontal emphasis of the typical medieval Cornish church. John Loughborough Pearson, the architect of the new cathedral, made one concession to Cornwall's churches by retaining the south aisle of 1504–18 from the old St Mary's church. This aisle is still one of the finest examples of Perpendicular display in Cornwall today, albeit in a damaged and partly restored state.

Internally, the cathedral is even more convincing as a two-thirds scale French cathedral. The tomb of John Robartes, whose son built Lanhydrock, can now be seen in the north transept of the cathedral, though originally in the parish church. Robartes was Truro's leading tin merchant. Earlier Truro tin merchants, including the Tregian family had

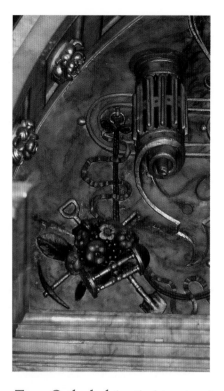

Truro Cathedral *detail of tin miners' tools from John Robartes' tomb of 1614. Kneeling figures from a similar tomb (of John Robartes' sister and her husband) can be seen in the Royal Cornwall Museum, Truro.*

paid for the 1518 glazing of the south aisle of Truro church before moving on to scale the Perpendicular heights with Probus tower.

Other religious denominations and their places of worship

Methodist chapels are today more common than churches (over 800 sites have been noted). Gwennap preaching pit is one of the more unusual Methodist sites. Equally picturesque is the thatched Quaker meeting house of 1710 at Come to Good, near Feock.

Gwennap Pit

Come to Good

unusual church building stories

Piracy and murder are among the more unusual stories relating to church building projects. St Anthony-in-Roseland was targeted by French pirates and burnt in 1338. The central tower with its spire and fine carved corbel heads therefore dates from after 1338. In 1595 Paul church suffered the same fate at the hands of the Spanish. The Spanish soldiers found an effigy of a horse in the church – probably part of the May Day troupe as at Padstow. The Polyphant pillars (brought from a quarry in Lewannick parish) of this exceptionally grand Penwith church were badly damaged by the fire and had to be replaced by octagonal granite piers. Lewannick's own Polyphant piers also failed to survive a fire in 1890.

At Linkinhorne the building of a south aisle may be linked to the murder of the vicar there in 1411. The south aisle is built of Tartendown stone brought from near Saltash and dates architecturally to 1400 or shortly after. The Botreaux family, one of the wealthiest in Cornwall, were

Linkinhorne interior with wall painting of Seven Acts of mercy. This shows how colourful Cornwall's churches may have been. A fragment of Romanesque capital may represent an earlier aisle removed with the building of the south aisle in about 1400.

Paul church showing the remains of the Polyphant piers at the junction between chancel and nave.

Egloskerry's back door with lindworm.

leading parishioners. The immediate cause of the murder was that the vicar Richard Peryn refused to let his parishioners have an extra priest. Probably this priest was needed to serve the new south chapel altar. Botreaux and more than twenty Linkinhorne parishioners complained to the bishop of Exeter in February 1411, but by March the vicar was dead. He had been murdered by unknown assasins while riding to Clampits to visit one of the complaining parishioners. All the bishop could do was record the murder in his register and excommunicate (exclude from all church services including burial) the unknown assailants who were termed 'Satellites of Satan'.

looking at cornish churches

While visitors to churches tend to look at the inside of a church first (the weather often being a major element here), architectural historians usually prefer to start with the outside. My own preference is to work from the inside out. The advantage of the 'inside-out' approach is that it immediately poses the question of how the church building was actually used through time. It also puts people in the picture and makes even the most restored church worth a look. Among the more unusual, or less well-known, things to look for in Cornish churches are the following in date order:

The glory of granite
St Neot, view of exterior from the west. Aside from Fairford in Gloucestershire, this parish church has the most complete medieval (restored 1820s) glazing scheme in Britain. It also has wonderful roofs (angels on the south side, original paintwork in the nave, and four fish roof bosses on the north). A fragmentary wall painting also survives as part of the saint's tomb, which doubled as the Easter Sepulchre.

A pair of rather beautiful facing lions appear on the Romanesque tympanum over the south door at Treneglos. Also of this period are the tympana at Egloskerry. The lamb and cross symbol of St John the Baptist formerly appeared above the south door, while a legless dragon or lindworm still appears over the 'devil's door' on the north. The three-headed font at Germoe may be the earliest in Cornwall and could well date from before the Norman Conquest. Cornwall has an exceptionally rich collection of Norman fonts, and a good example of an Early English font can be seen at St Erme.

The variety of Decorated period architecture can best be understood by contrasting St Ive chancel's lush ornateness with the plainness of Lostwithiel's clerestoried interior. Not to be missed are the carved tower corbel faces inside St Anthony-in-Roseland, or the man with toothache on St Columb Major's font.

To enjoy Perpendicular architecture in Cornwall one must love granite. Excellent

St Ives sandrock pier of north aisle. *This material was easier to carve than granite. Note the additional 'wave' moulding instead of the usual hollow chamfer. Piers with this section can also be seen at St Just-in-Penwith and Madron where limestone was used, and more commonly in Devon where it is known as Devon type B (type A being the equivalent of the Cornish standard Perpendicular pier).*

examples of granite ashlar work can be found at Advent, St Breward, St Buryan and St Neot amongst other places, with an over-abundance of carving at Launceston St Mary Magdalene. Other distinctive stones like limestone and Polyphant can sometimes be found in use, sandrock was used for piers at St Ives, Catacleuse at St Merryn and more selectively elsewhere in north Cornwall. The largest church (Bodmin at 150 feet in length) and the tallest tower (Probus at 123 feet 6 inches) also date from the Perpendicular period. This is the period of woodcarving par-excellence, especially bench-ends, which survive in more than a third of Cornish churches.

Angels, often clasping shields, occur in various places including the bench ends at Altarnun. Stone ones are found on fonts at Camborne, Gulval, and St Ives, amongst other places, and on pier capitals too in the latter two

Launcells early to mid–sixteenth century bench end of St Peter's sword and Malchus's ear.

Opposite
St Kew c1490 window detail showing St Peter cutting off Malchus's ear.

places. Stained-glass angels occur at St Kew and St Neot and in a wall-painting of the probable Easter sepulchre at Lanteglos-by-Fowey.

Passion symbols from the Life of Christ are a favourite subject for bench-ends and can be interesting to decode (J C D Smith's book *Church Woodcarvings; A West Country Study,* 1969, includes a list of the most common on pages 105–6). The full story of the Passion survives in stained glass at St Kew and also forms the second part of the Cornish language religious play known as the Ordinalia. Christ showed his wounds in stained glass and wall paintings and as a warning to Sabbath breakers in at least four places (the St Neot stained glass panel is now in the Royal Cornwall Museum, Truro). Tools relevant to the parish were often included – a boat in the case of St Just-in-Penwith. A most unusual bench-end survival is the pieta (St Mary with the dead Christ on her lap) at St Keverne.

Secular themes on bench ends include Reynard the Fox preaching to geese at Padstow, and to a foolish woman at St Austell. A camel and camel driver appear on a bench-end at St Columb Major and monkeys dance on the back of the rood screen at Mawgan-in-Pydar. Green men of all dates adorn several Cornish roof bosses, the best dragons are on the screen base at St Eval. At Altarnun, a sword dancer is the subject on two bench ends.

Altarnun bench end the second of the sword dancer panels, 1530s. In the first panel the dancer holds the sword above his head.

fURthER REAÖING:

A useful booklist is included in Charles Thomas & Joanna Mattingly, *The History of Christianity in Cornwall AD 500–2000*, published by the Royal Institution of Cornwall, Truro in 2000. This list does not include Eamon Duffy's, *The Voices of Morebath* (Yale & London, 2001), which focuses on the impact of the Reformation on one north Devon community or *Changes and Chances* the Cornwall Historic Churches Trust's 50th anniversary publication.

acknowleÖGments:

I am grateful to Eric Berry, Jo Cox, Bernard Deacon, John Gould, Alex Hooper, Andrew Langdon, Harold Mattingly, Nicholas Orme, Oliver Padel, Ann Preston-Jones, David Rhymer, and David Thomas for reading and commenting on earlier drafts of this booklet and Charles Thomas for discussing some aspects. I would also like to thank former students especially Margaret Wade who many years ago said that she would never look at a church the same way again. Any mistakes here are my own.

North door of St Ervan church which may date from the Victorian restoration or later. Note the gravestone acting as buttress.